THE CATHOLIC FAITH

A Summary Statement
Based on the Australian Catechism
and revised in the light of the
Catechism of the Catholic Church

Compiled by Bishop Peter J. Elliott

NEW REVISED EDITION
FREEDOM PUBLISHING BOOKS
2021

Published in Australia by
Freedom Publishing Books
33 Scoresby Road
Bayswater VIC 3153

Nihil Obstat:	Rev. Dr Cameron Forbes STD
	Diocesan Censor
Imprimatur:	Very Reverend Joseph Caddy AM Lic.Soc.Sci VG
	Vicar General
	Archdiocese of Melbourne
Date:	30 September 2021

The Nihil Obstat and Imprimatur are official declarations that a book or pamphlet is free of doctrinal or moral error. No implication is contained therein that those who have granted the Nihil Obstat and Imprimatur agree with the contents, opinions or statements expressed. They do not necessarily signify that the work is approved as a basic text for catechetical instruction.

***

ISBN 9781922589088

Catalogue-in-Publication entry is available from the National Library of Australia http://catalogue.nla.gov.au

Printed by Brougham Press

Introduction

This book is a basic statement of the Catholic faith. It may assist in the formation of both older children and adults. It includes common Catholic prayers, which might well be memorised, together with Scripture references so that it can be studied with a Bible.

Since 1974, when it was first published as a pamphlet by the Australian Catholic Truth Society, *The Catholic Faith* has been reprinted sixteen times and revised twice. The last printing of the original edition (1987) was published by the Society of St Vincent de Paul, followed by a revised edition published by the Society of St Peter Canisius in 1996. A Chinese translation was recently published in the Archdiocese of Kuching, Malaysia.

The Catholic Faith has thus proved to be Australia's most widely used compact summary of the faith. It has introduced inquirers to Catholicism and helped catechumens and converts to believe and live the eternal truths of Christ's Church.

This latest edition is still based on the *Australian Catechism* (1937), revised in the light of the Second Vatican Council. However, following the *Catechism of the Catholic Church* (published in English in 1994), the sections have been re-arranged and much new material has been included. An Appendix has been added so that this basic statement, which is not an official catechism, may now serve as a key to the deeper and more detailed content of the *Catechism of the Catholic Church*.

† PJE

Contents

PART I. WE BELIEVE

God reveals Himself to us through his deeds and words. Through my mind and will, I respond to God and I believe in Him and his revealed truths. This is **Faith**.

We cannot be saved without faith. Faith is a gift of God.

1. FAITH AND REVELATION

God has revealed Himself and called men and women to a life of faith in gradual stages. First He revealed Himself to his chosen People Israel, through saving events and holy prophets. Then He revealed Himself to us in the deeds and words of his Son Jesus Christ, who founded the Catholic Church.

We know the content of this Revelation through the Church. Guided by the Holy Spirit, Christ's Church teaches **doctrines of faith**, what we are to believe, and **doctrines of morals**, how we are to live.

Doctrines of faith and morals are revealed in the Bible and in Tradition. Together, the Bible with Tradition make up God's Revelation to us.

The Bible and Tradition

By the *Bible*, or Scriptures, we mean the Books of the New Testament and of the Old Testament which, as they were written under the inspiration of the Holy Spirit, have God as their Author. We should read the Bible because the Church put it together as her own library of holy books.

However, the Bible does not contain all the truths given to us under the inspiration of the Holy Spirit. Some of these truths are contained in Tradition. St. Paul says: "**So then,** brethren, stand firm and hold to the traditions which you were taught by us, either by word of mouth or by letter" (2 Thessalonians 2:15).

By "Tradition" we mean those teachings of Christ which were not written in the books of the Bible and have come down to us within the Catholic Church through the Apostles and their successors, the Pope and the Bishops.

2. PRINCIPAL TRUTHS OF CHRISTIAN REVELATION

We can know God on earth:

1. by seeing the wonderful things God has made and
2. by learning the truths God has taught.

We know what God has taught from the teachings of his Church which is "**the pillar and defence of the truth**" (1 Timothy 3:15).

We can understand many of the truths which God has revealed, but there are some truths which we cannot fully understand. These are called Mysteries of Religion.

The chief Mysteries of Religion are the Holy Trinity and the Incarnation (see No. 5).

The Holy Trinity

The Mystery of the Holy Trinity means that in one God there are really three distinct Persons, equal in all things, and having only one and the same Divine Nature.

The First Person is **God the Father**, the Second Person is **God the Son**, and the Third Person is **God the Holy Spirit**.

Christians are baptized "In the name of the Father and of the Son and of the Holy Spirit" (Matthew 28:19 and see No. 14).

The Holy Trinity is revealed through Jesus Christ. He is God the Son made man. He called God his Father and he promised that the Holy Spirit would come to us (Mark 14: 36; John 14:25, 26).

To understand why Jesus Christ became one of us, we must first understand God's plan of creation and how sin entered the world.

"I BELIEVE IN GOD THE FATHER ALMIGHTY, CREATOR OF HEAVEN AND EARTH."

3. GOD THE CREATOR: OUR DESTINY

God made everything. He created everything; that is, He made it out of nothing. God is the Creator of the world, the sun and moon, the planets and the stars (Genesis 1). God is the living Being without beginning and without end. God is infinitely great and infinitely good.

There is only one God. He is in heaven, on earth, and everywhere, but we do not see God because God is a Spirit, having no body (John 4: 24). Therefore, God cannot be seen by us in this life.

God sees us and always watches over us, because He loves us (Matthew 10:29-31; Wisdom 11:24-26). God can do all things. God made the world to show his love, his power and wisdom, and to help us to reach our home in heaven.

With the help of my parents, God made me, giving me a body and soul. God created my soul, and He made me like Himself. I am like God because:

1. I have a spirit;
2. I will never die;
3. I can know and love God.

4. OUR ORIGIN, THE FALL, THE ANGELS

In the beginning, God created man (Genesis 2). Man was created:

1. in the image of God; that is, as a person who can know and love.

2, as one person, body and soul, made of matter and spirit;

3. as male or female persons, made for each other;

4. to be good, holy, and happy on earth and in heaven.

However, we needed to be saved because our first parents, Adam and Eve, who had been created to enjoy God's kingdom of heaven, sinned against God and by their sin closed heaven against all human beings. In the story of our first parents, the name "Adam" means "man"; the name "Eve" means "woman"

We read that our first parents disobeyed God when He tested their obedience to Him, their Lord and Master (Genesis 3). In this way, the story teaches us the truth that God has created men and women with **free-will** (see No. 21).

By saying that God has created man with "free-will", we mean that God has given each of us the power to obey Him, or to disobey Him, not forcing us to be good.

God made our first parents free, but the devil tempted them because it wanted them to disobey God. The devil is one of the fallen angels.

The Angels

The angels are spirits like our souls, but they have no bodies. Like man and woman they were made free to choose so that they could win or lose heaven. God loved them too much to force them to be good. But the angels were so great and beautiful that some fell into the sin of pride. They rebelled against God and are punished in hell forever (Luke 10:18; 2 Peter 2:4; Revelation 12:7-9). These fallen angels are called devils or demons.

God rewarded the good angels by allowing them to see and serve Him in heaven, thus making them happy forever.

Each of us has a guardian angel to help us to serve God (Matthew 18:10).

After the Fall of Man and Woman

By their sin of rebellion and disobedience, our first parents lost the wonderful gift of Sanctifying Grace (see No. 27) and with it the right to heaven. In the story of Adam and Eve (Genesis 3), we read that they were driven out of the Garden of Eden and, with all their descendants to the end of the world, were doomed to die. In this way the story teaches us the truth that the sin of our first parents comes down to each of us.

We are born in **original sin**. By saying that we are "born in original sin" we mean that because of the sin of our first parents:

1. we are born without Sanctifying Grace and without a right to heaven;

2. we have an inclination to do wrong (commit sins);

3. we must suffer death and the pains and miseries of this life.

The Blessed Virgin Mary, and she alone, was conceived and born free from original sin. This favour from God is called her **Immaculate Conception**. God gave her this favour because she would be his Mother when, in his love, God became one of us.

God never abandoned us to sin but promised to send us a Saviour (Genesis 3:9,15). We must therefore understand how and why God Himself became one of us.

"I BELIEVE IN JESUS CHRIST, HIS ONLY SON, OUR LORD"

5. CHRIST AND HIS WORK FOR US

God the Son became one of us to rescue us from sin and to take us to be with him in heaven.

God the Son, when he became **Man**, was called **Jesus Christ**. His chosen name Jesus means in Hebrew "God saves". His title "Christ" means in Greek "anointed" from the Hebrew word "messiah". Because he is the only Son of God, who has conquered death and who reigns forever, "**Jesus is the Lord**".

The Incarnation and its Purpose

The Mystery of the **Incarnation** means that God the Son, the Second Person of the Holy Trinity, became Man.

The word "Incarnation" means "coming into flesh", because God the Son became Man, by taking, through the power of the Holy Spirit, a body and a soul like ours in the womb of the Blessed Virgin Mary (John 1:14).

God the Son became Man to save us (John 3:16, 17).

God the Son saved us when he completed his perfect life by his sufferings and death on the cross and by his glorious Resurrection (Philippians 2:5-11). This is known as the Paschal Mystery.

Jesus Christ, God and Man

Jesus Christ is true God and true Man. Jesus is truly God

because he is the Second Person of the Holy Trinity, and therefore he has one and the same Nature with God the Father and God the Holy Spirit.

Jesus Christ is **truly Man** because, while truly God, he has a complete human nature, that is, a body and a soul exactly like ours in all things, except sin (Hebrews 4:15).

But there is only *one Person* in Jesus Christ, and that Person is the Second Divine Person of the Holy Trinity.

There are two natures in Jesus Christ, a divine nature and a human nature. He is the God-Man.

In his divine nature, Jesus Christ could perform miracles. In his human nature, he could suffer and die for us.

Jesus Christ had no human father. God is his Father, but he has a human mother, the Blessed Virgin Mary.

The Life of Jesus Christ

On the day of the Annunciation, the Archangel Gabriel announced to the Blessed Virgin Mary, "... **behold you will conceive in your womb and bear a son, and you shall call his name Jesus.** " (Luke 1:31). When Mary said "yes", by the power of the Holy Spirit she conceived God the Son and became the Mother of God.

On Christmas Day, Jesus Christ was born of the Blessed Virgin in a stable at Bethlehem (Matthew 1,2; Luke 2; John 1:1-18).

When Jesus grew up, he left home and went around teaching people about his Father and the coming of the Kingdom of God. He gathered around him a group of followers (disciples) and to twelve of these (the Apostles) he gave special teaching and a share in his power, mission and authority. He performed miracles to show that he was

God. His miracles show us the power, love and care of God.

On Good Friday, Jesus Christ died, nailed to a cross, to redeem and save us (Matthew 26, 27; Mark 14, 15; Luke 22, 23; John 18, 19). We call this day "good" on which Jesus died because his death has shown how much he loves us and has brought us so many benefits. While the body of Jesus was in the tomb, his soul went to the souls of all good people who died before Christ; waiting until he would save them and take them to heaven (John 5:25; 1 Peter 4:6).

On Easter Sunday, the third day after his death, Jesus Christ arose, body and soul, glorious and immortal, from the dead (Matthew 28; Mark 16; Luke 24; John 20,21). Jesus Christ rose in the same human body that suffered on the cross, but his body was changed for a new life, no longer limited to our earthly time and space. He raised us by his Resurrection to that sharing in the divine life which is the life of Grace and the hope of our resurrection (see No. 11). The death of Jesus proves that he is Man and his Resurrection proves that he is God.

On Ascension Thursday, forty days after Easter, Jesus Christ passed body and soul into heaven (Matthew 28:16-20; Mark 16:19,20; Luke 24:50-53; Acts 1:1-11). He will come again with glory to judge the living and the dead (see No. 11).

"I BELIEVE IN THE HOLY SPIRIT"

6. THE HOLY SPIRIT

Jesus Christ promised that, after his Resurrection and Ascension, the **Holy Spirit** would come to those who believed in him (Luke 24: 49; John 14:16-18, 15:26, 16:7-11). The Holy Spirit is given to the sons and daughters who call God "Father" (Galatians 4:6). The Spirit can never be separated from the Son and the Father.

We believe in the Holy Spirit:

1. who inspires the Scriptures;
2. who is proclaimed in Tradition;
3. who guides the teaching Church (Magisterium);
4. who is present in our worship and prayer;
5. who imparts gifts and ministries in the Church;
6. who is at work in apostles, missionaries and saints.

The Holy Spirit is the "breath" of God; the Paraclete (consoler) (John 14:16,26, 15:26, 16:7), and the Spirit of Truth (John 16:13).

We can understand the work of the invisible Spirit through symbols: 1. water (John 4:17-14), 2. anointing (1 John 2:20), 3. fire (Luke 3:16; Acts 2:3-4), 4. Cloud and light (Exodus 40: 36-38; Luke 9:34-35), 5. a permanent seal (John 6:27; 2 Corinthians 1:22; Ephesians 1:13; 4:30), 6. the hands (Acts 8:17-19), 7. the finger (Exodus 31:18; 2 Corinthians 3:3), and 8. the dove (Mark 1:9-11).

The Work of the Holy Spirit

In the time of the promises, the Holy Spirit was at work in the creation of man and the universe, in calling Abraham and then in guiding and teaching God's People, Israel.

In the fullness of time, the Holy Spirit prepared the Blessed ever Virgin Mary and through the power of the Spirit she conceived God the Son, Emmanuel, "God-with-us" (Matthew 1:23). The Holy Spirit was always with Jesus, the Christ, God's anointed-One, the true Messiah.

In these last times, the Lord who died and rose again for us, promised that he would send us his Spirit.

On **Pentecost Sunday**, the Holy Spirit came down upon

the chosen followers of Jesus, his Apostles, in the form of flames of fire.

Jesus Christ sent the Holy Spirit to strengthen and enlighten his Apostles and to give life to the Church, guiding and guarding her, and making her holy through all ages.

"I BELIEVE IN THE HOLY CATHOLIC CHURCH"

7. CHRIST'S CHURCH

The word "Church" means the assembly of those called and gathered by God. Jesus the Good Shepherd gathers his own People, to teach, feed and save them.

We can understand the Church through symbols: 1. a sheepfold (John 10:1-16), 2. a cultivated field (Matthew 21:33-43), 3. God's household (Ephesians 2:19-22); 4. a building (1 Peter 2:5); 5. the bride of Christ. (Ephesians 5:25-32; Revelation 21:9), 6. our mother above, the new Jerusalem (Galatians 4: 26; Revelation 21:2).

Founded by Christ

Jesus Christ came on earth not only to die for us, but also to teach us what we must believe and do to save our souls. To save our souls; we must believe in Jesus Christ and all his teaching, for **"without faith it is impossible to please Him"** (Hebrews 11:6). In faith, we must do good, **"For as the body apart from the spirit is dead, so faith apart from works is dead."** (James 2:6).

Jesus Christ founded a visible society, the Church, to give us his teaching and to guide and help us on our pilgrim way to heaven.

We must believe the teaching of the Church, because the

Church has authority from Jesus Christ to teach. Jesus said to his Apostles, "**All authority in heaven and on earth has been given to me. Go therefore and make disciples of all nations, baptizing them in the name of the Father and of the Son and of the Holy Spirit, teaching them to observe all that I have commanded you; and behold, I am with you always, to the close of the age.**" (Matthew 28:18-20).

The Unfailing Church

Jesus Christ promised that the Church he founded would last for all time. He said, "**and I tell you, you are Peter, and on this rock I will build my church, and the powers of death shall not prevail against it.**" (Matthew 16:18).

The Church Christ founded exists both in time and eternity. She is both human and divine. On earth, she is a visible structure with different levels, a "hierarchy". She is a "sacrament", the sign and instrument of our salvation.

Through faith, we can understand this Mystery of the Church in three ways: 1. the **People of God**, 2. the **Body of Christ** and 3. the **Temple of the Holy Spirit**.

1. The People of God

God the Father forms the Church to be one family and one People of God: "**You are a chosen race, a royal priesthood, God's own people.**" (1 Peter 2:9). We enter God's People through faith and Baptism.

God's People make up a visible society, a distinct people, a holy nation, destined to become the fullness of the Kingdom of God.

2. The Body of Christ

God the Son, our Lord Jesus Christ, is united to his body the Church and she draws her life from him.

The Church can never be separated from him. Christ is the Head of his Body, the Church (Colossians 1:18; Ephesians 5:23). By Baptism, we are made members of this Mystical Body of Christ (Romans 6:4-5; 1 Corinthians 12:13; and see n. 14). Many members with different functions and gifts make up the Body of Christ (1 Corinthians 12). But all grow as one Body through sharing in the one Eucharist (see No. 16).

Christ is the Bridegroom who gives himself for his beloved Bride, the Church (Ephesians 5:25-32), so that she may become our fruitful Mother.

3. The Temple of the Holy Spirit

God the Holy Spirit is the "soul" of the Mystical Body of Christ.

The Holy Spirit is the source of the life and unity, and of all the different gifts within the Church. All members of the Church are living temples of the Holy Spirit (1 Corinthians 6:19) and are called to be holy (see No. 27) The special gifts the Holy Spirit gives to members of the Body of Christ are called "charisms".

The Church is the work of the Holy Trinity. God the Father calls us into the Body of his Son, where we are filled with the Holy Spirit.

8. THE MARKS OF THE TRUE CHURCH

The true Church founded by Jesus Christ is the Holy Catholic Church. This true Church is found in the People who are governed by the Pope, and the Bishops in union with him.

Christ's words and our own reason tell us that there are four chief marks or signs by which the true Church can be known. The true Church is: 1. **One**; 2. **Holy**; 3. **Catholic**, that is, universal; 4. **Apostolic**. The Catholic Church alone is one, holy, universal and apostolic, and is therefore the one true Church of Jesus Christ.

1. **One**: The Catholic Church is one because all God's People believe the same truths, offer to God the same Holy Sacrifice, share the same Sacraments and are united under one visible head on earth, the Pope.

We pray and work for unity, so that separated Christians, who are not full members of the Church, and people of other religions will be drawn into the perfect unity of the Church, as Christ wills (John 17:20-23).

2. **Holy**: The Catholic Church is holy because she was founded by Jesus Christ and through her holy teaching and the Sacraments she gives us all the graces that in every age make men and women remarkable for holiness. Such people are the saints.

We find the perfect holiness of the Church in Mary ever Virgin, the first of all believers, who now reigns as Queen of Heaven (Revelation 12:1-6; 13-17).

3. **Catholic or Universal**: The Catholic Church is universal because her Founder, Jesus Christ, sent her to teach all nations. Everywhere and in every age, she teaches everything that Jesus taught. Men and women of all races belong to God's People and anyone can join the Church.

Everyone is bound to belong to the Catholic Church because Our Lord said to his Apostles, "**Go into all the world and preach the gospel to all creation. He who believes and**

**is baptized will be saved; but he who does not believe will
be condemned."** (Mark 16:15, 16).

Those who deliberately and through their own fault are outside the Catholic Church cannot be saved. However, those who through no fault of their own are outside the Catholic Church will be saved, if they die in the state of grace, that is, following their consciences and trying to be good.

We understand that the Church is Catholic as we become part of her mission to bring the truth, salvation, peace and justice of Christ to all people everywhere.

4. **Apostolic**: The Catholic Church is apostolic because she holds the truths taught by the Apostles and because the Bishops of the Catholic Church can trace back their authority in an unbroken line to Jesus Christ and the Apostles.

We understand that the Church is apostolic by following and obeying our beloved Pope and Bishops, the pastors Jesus Christ has given us.

9. THE MEMBERS OF THE CHURCH

The members of the Church are our Holy Father the Pope, and with him all the Bishops, clergy and people who are baptized and who recognize the Pope to be the Vicar (deputy) of Christ on earth and the visible head of God's People.

The Pope and Bishops

The Pope is the successor of St. Peter, who was chief of the Apostles, Christ's Vicar (deputy) on earth, and first Pope and Bishop of Rome.

We know St Peter was made the visible head of the Church because Jesus said to him, "**And I tell you, you are**

Peter, and on this rock I will build my church, and the powers of death shall not prevail against it. I will give you the keys of the kingdom of heaven, and whatever you bind on earth shall be bound in heaven, and whatever you loose on earth shall be loosed in heaven." (Matthew 16:18,19).

After the resurrection, Jesus Christ appointed St Peter shepherd over his whole flock, when he said, "**Feed my lambs... feed my sheep.**" (John 21:15-17). The Successors of the other Apostles are all the other Bishops of the Catholic Church. Together with the Pope, they make up one apostolic "college" (united group) to teach, sanctify (make holy) and govern God's People.

Helped by their priests and deacons, Bishops are ordained to serve and lead God's People (see No. 19). They all receive authority and power to teach, to sanctify and to govern God's People. Most Bishops care for a particular Church (the diocese). Together, all these local Churches make up the one Catholic Church on earth. With the Pope, all the Bishops share in the care of the whole Church.

Most local Churches belong to the Latin (Roman or Western) Rite, but some belong to an Eastern Rite (Ukrainian, Maronite, Melkite, Chaldean, Syro-Malabar). In communion with the Pope and Latin Bishops, these **Eastern Churches** are a major part of the Catholic Church.

The Teaching Church

The voice of the teaching Church is called the **Magisterium**.

The Church cannot make a mistake in teaching, for Jesus promised the Pastors of his Church that he would send the Holy Spirit, the Spirit of Truth, to teach them all truth and to remain with them forever. "**And I will pray the Father,** and He will give you another Counselor, to be with you forever." (John 14:16) "When the Spirit of Truth comes he will guide you into all truth, for he will not speak of his own authority but whatever he hears he will speak, and he will declare to you the things that are to come" (John 16:13).

By the infallibility of the Pope, we mean that the Pope cannot teach what is false when, speaking as Head of the Church, he defines doctrines of faith and morals.

By the infallibility of the Church, we mean that the Bishops and the Pope gathered in a General Council of the Church, cannot teach what is false when together they define doctrines of faith and morals.

We are bound to accept not only infallibly defined doctrines, but other teaching clearly given to us through the Magisterium of the Pope and Bishops.

Christ's Faithful

Most members of the Church are the laity (from the Greek for "people") or lay faithful because they are baptized believers. They have not received Holy Orders. Through Baptism, the laity share in the priesthood of Christ in their own way. They are called and empowered to carry out the mission of Jesus Christ where they live and work in the world (see No. 14)

As faithful laity in the world, we share in the three offices of Jesus Christ who is Prophet, Priest and King:

1. we are a priestly People, called to offer God perfect worship;

2. we are a prophetic People, believing and proclaiming God's truth;

3. we are a kingly People, as we serve others in Christ's name.

Lay faithful work in union with their pastors as they carry out their mission in the world.

Some members of the Church are called to serve God and others in **consecrated life**. They promise to live according to Christ's special Gospel call, in poverty, chastity and obedience. Most men and women who live different forms of the consecrated life are monks, nuns, brothers, sisters, hermits or members of lay institutes.

Other Christians

All who have been baptized and follow Jesus Christ outside the Catholic Church have the right to be called Christians. By baptism they have some, though imperfect, form of union with the Catholic Church.

The Eastern Orthodox Churches (Greek, Russian etc.) are closest to the Catholic Church, because they believe most Catholic doctrines and because they have true bishops and seven sacraments.

The Protestants and Anglicans have different forms of ministry and sacraments, with doctrines based mainly on their understanding of the Bible. We pray and work with other Christians, so that one day we may share fully in Catholic unity (see No. 8).

"I BELIEVE IN THE COMMUNION OF THE SAINTS."

10. THE COMMUNION OF SAINTS

The Church is a "communion" in which all members share the benefits of the faith, the sacraments, their spiritual gifts and mutual love.

In this life and the next, holy Church exists in three forms:

1. **militant**, in her pilgrim members struggling here on earth;

2. **expectant**, in her members being purified in purgatory,

3. **triumphant**, in her members who enjoy the glory of God forever in heaven.

By the Communion of Saints, we also mean that the members of the Church on earth, the souls in purgatory and the saints in heaven are all united as the one family of God. We can all help one another in this great family of God.

We should ask the prayers of the Blessed Virgin Mary and the saints, because they are God's friends, united with us through the Communion of Saints.

Mary, Mother of Christ, Mother of the Church

The Blessed Virgin Mary can never be separated from her Son. He gave her to us to be our Mother when he was dying on the cross (John 19:26-27). Our Lady encouraged the early Church by her prayers (Acts 1:14). She is thus the Mother of all believers.

Raised up, body and soul, the Blessed Virgin Mary already enjoys the glory of heaven. This favour from God is called her Assumption.

The Church teaches us to pray frequently to the Blessed Virgin because she is the Mother of God and Mother of the Church, and therefore has special power in heaven (see Prayers, No. 33).

"WE BELIEVE IN THE RESURRECTION OF THE BODY AND LIFE EVERLASTING."

11. DEATH: HEAVEN: PURGATORY: HELL: JUDGEMENT
The Resurrection of the Body means that we shall all rise

again on the last day with the same bodies that we had in this life, but our bodies will be glorified, made perfect and new, like the risen Lord Jesus (1 Corinthians 15).

Life everlasting means that we are immortal beings, who will be raised up by God to the eternal life of the risen Lord Jesus (Matthew 23:31-32; John 11:23-26).

What we believe and do in this life determines what awaits us after death. The four **Last Things** to be ever remembered are: Death, Heaven, Hell and Judgement.

1. Death

Death came into the world because of original sin (see No. 4). By rising again in our human flesh, the Lord Jesus has conquered death (Romans 5:19-21; 6:3-9; 1 Corinthians 15:54-57).

At death, our life is changed, not ended. Trusting in Jesus Christ, we should not fear death (Philippians 1:21). At death my soul is separated from my body, which decays. I only die once (Hebrews 9:27); I have only one life in this world. There is no "reincarnation" after death.

I should pray for the grace to prepare for my death by prayer and repentance.

Immediately after death, my soul has to face my **Particular Judgement** which determines at once whether I am saved or lost forever (Luke 16:22,23). The sentence then passed will be confirmed by Jesus Christ, our Redeemer and Judge, on the last day, the Day of General Judgement.

2. Heaven

Jesus Christ has promised a place in heaven for those who believe in him (John 14:1-7). He will say to the good on the last day, "**Come, blessed of my Father, inherit the kingdom prepared for you from the foundation of the world.**" (Matthew 25:34).

Risen and glorified, the good will enter, both body and soul, into the perfect happiness of heaven, where they will be able to recognize and know one another.

Our reward in heaven will be the Blessed Vision of God. Then we shall see God's wondrous Glory, share his infinite Knowledge and Life, and together we will rejoice in his unchanging happiness forever.

At their Particular Judgement those who die in venial sin (see No. 24) go to **purgatory**.

Purgatory is a state of purification where some souls have to wait because they are not yet fit to go to heaven. Not only those who die in venial sin, but also those who have not done sufficient penance for sin forgiven, are sent to purgatory.

We can help the souls in purgatory by our prayers and good works, by gaining indulgences for them (see No. 17), and especially by the offering of the holy Sacrifice of the Mass. "**It is therefore a holy and wholesome thought to pray for the dead, that they may be loosed from their sins.**" (2 Maccabees 12:46).

All the souls in purgatory pass on to heaven, because God is preparing them to be with Him forever.

3. Hell

However, Jesus Christ will say to the wicked on the last day, "**Depart from me you cursed, into the eternal fire prepared for the devil and his angels.**" (Matthew 25:41). The wicked will go, both body and soul, into the everlasting punishment of hell fire (Matthew 10:28; 13:40-42; Mk 9:43-48). The main punishment of hell is the loss of God for ever.

4. Judgement

By the "Day of General Judgement" we mean that last day when, Jesus Christ taught, "**the Son of man is to come, with his angels in the glory of his Father, and then he will repay everyone for what he or she has done.**" (Matthew 16:27). On the last day, Christ will come to judge us with great power and majesty and all the angels with him. We shall all appear before the tribunal of God in our own bodies to give an account of our deeds (Revelation 20:11-15).

The New Heaven and the New Earth

At the end of time, the Kingdom of God will come in its fullness and the Church will be perfected and triumphant. Glorified in body and soul, the just will reign for ever and the material universe itself will be transformed.

God will then be "**all in all**" (1 Corinthians 15:28).

To this, our Catholic Faith, we say: "**Yes, we believe — Amen!**"

Part II. WE WORSHIP AND CELEBRATE

12. THE LITURGY

God calls us to offer worship to Him. Divine worship. is called the Liturgy, meaning our public duty or service. In celebrating the Liturgy we share in the work of Jesus Christ, through worship, prayer and listening to God's word.

The Holy Spirit works within us when we celebrate the Liturgy of Jesus Christ, our, great High Priest (Hebrews 4:4-16). In the Liturgy, the Mass and the Sacraments build the Church, deepen our faith, and bring us salvation and eternal life.

The **Mass** and the **Sacraments** are celebrated through the signs and symbols of the Liturgy of the Church. We worship God through words and actions, singing and music, assisted by holy images and following sacred times and seasons.

We celebrate the Mass, especially on Sunday, the first day of the week, the Day of Our Lord's. Resurrection. We gather in a church, at an altar dedicated for sacred worship. The church is a house of prayer where we celebrate and receive the Sacraments.

13, THE SACRAMENTS

A Sacrament is an external human action chosen by Christ to give us Grace. All the Sacraments give us Sanctifying Grace and each Sacrament gives a right to special actual graces (see No. 27).

Christ gave his Church **seven Sacraments**:

1. Baptism; 2. Confirmation; 3. Blessed Eucharist; 4. Penance;

5. Anointing of the Sick; 6. Holy Orders; 7. Matrimony.

Three of these Sacraments give a spiritual mark or seal to the soul, the "character" that cannot be removed, and so they cannot be repeated: Baptism, Confirmation and Holy Orders.

The three **Sacraments of Christian Initiation** are Baptism, Confirmation and the Eucharist. These are the Sacraments of birth and growth in the life of faith.

14. BAPTISM

The **Sacrament of Baptism** cleanses us from original sin by giving us Sanctifying Grace. Born again and made inwardly good and holy, we become the children of God and members of Christ's Mystical Body, the Church.

The Church is called the "Mystical Body of Christ" because all of God's People through Baptism are joined together in one Body with Christ as head, and all share his new Life by Sanctifying Grace (see No. 7 and No. 27).

In Baptism we receive the gift of faith. The Church baptizes both those who can profess the faith and infants who will grow in the gift of faith.

Baptism is given by pouring water on the head of the person to be baptized, or by immersing the person in water, saying at the same time: "I baptize you in the name of the Father and of the Son and of the Holy Spirit."

We cannot go to heaven without Baptism. Jesus Christ said, "**Truly, truly, I say to you, unless one is born of water and the Spirit, one cannot enter the Kingdom of God.**" (John 3:5).

However, either martyrdom for the Faith or an act or perfect love of God can take the place of Baptism of water. A martyr is a person who dies for his or her faith in Jesus Christ (Revelation 7:14-17). All infants who die without Baptism go to be happy with God for ever.

The permanent "character" of Baptism gives us the lay form of the priesthood of Jesus Christ, with the power, right and duty to share in the worship and Sacraments of his holy Church.

15. CONFIRMATION

The **Sacrament of Confirmation** gives us the Gifts of the Holy Spirit in their fullness, and courage and strength to live always as sons and daughters of the Father and faithful disciples and soldiers of Jesus Christ. Together with Baptism and the Eucharist, this sacrament completes our initiation as Christians (Acts 8:15-17, 19:5-6, Hebrews 6:2).

We show ourselves faithful disciples and soldiers of Jesus Christ by always being ready to fight and to suffer for our Faith, even if necessary giving our lives for it. Jesus Christ promised, **"So every one who acknowledges me before men, I also will acknowledge before my Father who is in heaven."**(Matthew 10:32).

The Gifts of the Holy Spirit we receive in Confirmation are:

1. Wisdom; **2. Understanding**; **3. Counsel**; **4. Fortitude**;
5. Knowledge; **6. Piety**; **7. Fear of the Lord** (see No. 23).

The Sacrament of Confirmation is given by the Bishop or his representative priest. He anoints the forehead of the person to be confirmed with Sacred Chrism (the most important Holy Oil) and says, "(Name) be sealed with the Gift of the Holy Spirit."

The permanent "character" of Confirmation perfects the common priesthood the faithful receive in Baptism, and gives the confirmed person power to profess faith in Christ publicly on behalf of the Church (Ephesians 1:13, 4:30).

The faithful who bear this seal of the Spirit will be protected and claimed by God at the last day (Revelation 1:2-3, 9:4).

16. BLESSED EUCHARIST: SACRIFICE AND SACRAMENT

The Blessed Eucharist is the **Sacrifice** of the New Law, and its greatest Sacrament, for in the Eucharist, under the appearances of bread and wine, Our Lord Jesus Christ is present, is offered, and is received.

At the last Supper, the night before he was crucified, Jesus Christ took bread and blessed, and broke it, and gave it to his Apostles saying, "**Take, eat, this is my body,**" and he took the cup, and when he had given thanks he gave it to them saying, "**Drink of it, all of you, for this is my blood of the covenant which is poured out for many for the forgiveness of sins.**" And he added "**Do this in memory of me**" (Matthew 26:26-28; Luke 22:19).

When Our Lord spoke the words of consecration, "**This is my Body... This is my Blood**" the substance of the bread and wine was changed into his own Body and Blood, and only the appearances of bread and wine remained.

By the words "**Do this in memory of me**" Our Lord:

1. ordained his Apostles bishops and priests;

2. gave them power to ordain other bishops and priests;

3. commanded all priests in the same way and with the same words to consecrate, offer and give his Body and Blood.

A priest is a man who, through the Sacrament of Holy

Orders, has received special powers to carry on the work of Jesus Christ, and in particular to offer the Holy Sacrifice to God, with and for God's People (see No. 19).

The Eucharist, The Sacrifice

Sacrifice is the highest act of religion, in which a priest offers a victim to God, to acknowledge God's supreme dominion over us and our total dependence on Him and to establish union with God for our benefit.

A priest offers Sacrifice in the Mass when, acting in the Person of Jesus Christ, he uses the power of consecration which changes bread and wine into Our Lord's Body and Blood. The bread and wine are changed by the Holy Spirit into the Body and Blood of Jesus Christ at the consecration, during the Eucharistic Prayer. By "Body" and "Blood" we mean that the whole Christ is present under either of the appearances of bread and wine.

Therefore, Jesus Christ is present with us in the tabernacle, where the Blessed Sacrament is reserved in our churches. We should visit Jesus and pray to him there.

The Mass is the true **Sacrifice** of **the New Law** for in it our Lord Jesus Christ, through the priest, offers himself to the God the Father for the living and the dead.

The Mass is the same Sacrifice as that of the Cross because, in the Mass, Our Lord Himself is both Priest and Victim. Although he does not suffer or shed his blood again, he continues the one perfect Offering he made on the Cross.

We go to Mass to offer sacrifice to God, that is, to be united to Him. Those who, without good reason, miss Mass on Sundays and Holy Days of Obligation commit a mortal sin. Since the offering of Mass is the holiest act we can perform, it is good to go to Mass as often as we can.

When offering the Mass, we should unite our intentions with those of Our Lord:

1. to praise God;
2. to thank God for his gifts;
3. to offer reparation for our sins;
4. to ask God for all we need in soul and body.

To assist at Mass, we join with the priest and God's People assembled in offering the Divine Victim to God the Father, as though we were all present at the Sacrifice on Calvary. First we hear God's word, and then we celebrate his Sacrifice.

The most perfect way of sharing in his Holy Sacrifice is to receive the Lord Jesus in Holy Communion.

The Eucharist, The Sacrament

The Blessed Eucharist is the greatest Sacrament as well as the Sacrifice of Christ and his Church. It is God's greatest gift to us, as well as our greatest offering to God. It is the summit and source of the life of the Church.

In the Sacrament of the Blessed Eucharist:

1. we receive Jesus Christ, true God and true Man;
2. the Giver of all good gifts becomes the Food of our soul;
3. we depend on God for our life of Grace.

We call this Sacrament the "Eucharist" because it is an action of thanksgiving to God, and "Holy Communion" because it unites us to Christ in a real union (John 6:32-59) and makes us one body in him (1 Corinthians 10:16-17).

Before we receive Holy Communion we must be in a state of grace (with no mortal sin unconfessed), observe the fast (one hour before Communion), and we should make acts of Faith, Hope and Charity (see Prayers, No. 32 and No. 35).

In this sacred banquet, Christ is received as our food, the memory of his Passion is renewed, the soul is filled with Grace and a pledge of the eternal life to come is given to us.

The two **Sacraments of Healing** are Penance and Reconciliation and the Anointing of the Sick. These are the Sacraments that heal and free us from sin and suffering.

17. PENANCE AND RECONCILIATION

The Sacrament of Penance forgives the sins we commit after Baptism. Because it restores us to the friendship of God and the community of the Church it is also called the Sacrament of **Reconciliation**. It gives us a special grace to avoid sin and resist temptation.

Sins are forgiven by the power of God, which Jesus Christ gave to the priests of his Church when he said to his apostles: "**Receive the Holy Spirit. If your forgive the sins of any they are forgiven; if you retain the sins of any they are retained.**" (John 20: 22,23).

The four parts of the Sacrament of Penance are:

1. Contrition; 2. Confession; 3. Absolution; 4. Satisfaction.

1. **Contrition** is a heartfelt sorrow for having offended God, with a firm resolution of sinning no more. It may either be **Perfect Contrition** or **Imperfect Contrition**.

We should be sorry for our sins because they are an insult to God our Creator, who is infinitely loving, good and perfect, and because the Son of God was tortured and crucified for our sins. This sorrow is called Perfect Contrition (see No. 24).

Other reasons for Contrition are the fear of hell, the loss of heaven and the wickedness of sin. This sorrow is called Imperfect Contrition. It is not as good as Perfect Contrition.

A person who is in danger of death and who cannot go

to Confession should make an act of Perfect Contrition (See Prayers, No. 32).

2. **Confession** is telling our sins to the priest in order to have them forgiven by Jesus Christ. Before we go to Confession we should ask God for the Grace to make a good confession; we should carefully examine our conscience; we should make acts of contrition and resolve sincerely to sin no more (See **Prayers**, No. 34).

Those who deliberately conceal a mortal sin in Confession commit a grave sin by telling a lie to the Holy Spirit. Their confession is bad and must be made all over again.

3. **Absolution** is the pardon given by the priest, acting as minister of God in the Sacrament of Penance. He says, "I absolve you from your sins... " As he says these words to us, he represents Jesus Christ who truly forgives our sins.

Absolution is the most important moment in this Sacrament of Reconciliation with God and with his People, the Church.

4. **Satisfaction** is reparation (paying back, repairing) to God for sin. When we perform the penance we receive in Confession, we make satisfaction. These acts help us to share in the infinite and perfect satisfaction offered by Our Lord for all sins.

The Sacrament of Penance is given by a priest, who has been authorized by the Bishop to hear confessions and grant absolution.

Indulgences

The Church helps us in making reparation by granting indulgences. An indulgence is a remission (or pardon) through the power of the Church of the temporal punishment due to sin, after its guilt has been forgiven. The Church has power, to give indulgences because Jesus Christ promised: "**I will give you the keys of the kingdom of heaven and whatever you bind on earth shall be bound in heaven, and whatever you loose on earth shall be loosed in heaven.**" (Matthew 16:19).

A **Plenary Indulgence** remits all the penance owing for sins. A **Partial Indulgence** remits part of the penance owing for sins. We gain indulgences by saying the prayers or doing the works prescribed by the Church. We must be in a state of grace, and must carry out the conditions specially required, such as, Confession, Holy Communion, a visit to a church, or prayers for the Pope's intentions.

We cannot gain indulgences without Faith, by which we pray that God will accept the devotion or action which the Church provides in place of penance for sins. We can pray that indulgences we may gain may be given over to help the holy souls in Purgatory.

18. THE ANOINTING OF THE SICK

The **Sacrament of the Anointing of the Sick** is the way Jesus Christ unites the sick to the saving and healing power of his Cross. Our Lord sent his Apostles to anoint the sick (Mark 6:13). The early Church valued this Sacrament (James 5.14-15). Since Confession and Holy Communion usually accompany this healing Sacrament, we should receive it, if possible, when we are seriously ill and before we are in extreme danger of death.

The Sacrament of the Anointing of the Sick is given by a priest. He anoints the forehead and hands of the sick person with the Oil of the Sick, praying that he or she may be helped by the Grace of the Holy Spirit, freed from sin, saved and raised up.

This healing Sacrament gives grace and strength to the soul of the person who is ill. It also remits sin and may even restore bodily health if God so wills.

After they have received the Anointing of the Sick, those who are about to leave this life receive the Eucharist as their Viaticum or "food for the journey".

The two **Sacraments at the Service of Communion** are Holy Orders and Matrimony. These are Sacraments for specific vocations and missions in Christian life.

19. HOLY ORDERS

The **Sacrament of Holy Orders** gives Bishop and Priests the power to offer the Holy Sacrifice of the Mass, to forgive sin in the Sacrament of Penance, and to preach and teach with the authority of the Church. There are three Orders of ministry: Bishop, Priest and Deacon.

The special work of a **Bishop** is to teach with authority, to govern the particular Church (the diocese) which the Pope has entrusted to him, and to give the Sacraments of Holy Orders and Confirmation.

The special work of a **Priest** is first to preach and teach the Good News of Christ, and most importantly, to celebrate Mass and hear confessions. The Bishop sends the Priest to work in a particular place, and he gives him permission to use the powers of the Sacrament of Holy Orders.

The special work of a **Deacon** is to help the Bishop or a Priest, by preaching and teaching, by giving Holy Communion, by baptizing and assisting at marriages. The Bishop sends the Deacon to work in a particular place, and he gives him permission to use the powers of the Sacrament of Holy Orders.

The Sacrament of Holy Orders is given by the Bishop. He lays his hands on the candidate's head and then he prays that God will consecrate him for the ministry to which he is being ordained.

The Church is only able to ordain men, because Jesus Christ only ordained men and his priests represent him, the Bridegroom of the Church.

The Sacrament of Holy Orders permanently consecrates men to be Bishops, Priests and Deacon. With this character they receive the Grace of the Holy Spirit to carry out all their special duties as servants of God's People (2 Timothy 1:6).

20. MATRIMONY

The **Sacrament of Matrimony** (Marriage) unites husband and wife in a holy and inseparable union, derived from the perfect union between Jesus Christ and his beloved bride the Church.(Ephesians 5:21-33)

In the beginning God created man and woman and gave them to one another in marriage. Jesus Christ raised this natural kind of marriage to become a sacrament of his new Covenant. However, not all are meant to marry, because some Christians are called to a life of virginity or celibacy for the sake of God's Kingdom (Matt. 19:3-12).

A baptized man and woman give the Sacrament of Marriage to one another when they freely consent to marry. They must make this mutual consent before a priest, deacon or another authorized representative of the Church and at least two other witnesses.

Marriages of Catholics before a civil celebrant may be valid in civil law, but they are not valid in the sight of God.

An inter-Church marriage or "mixed marriage" is one between a Catholic and a non-Catholic. The Church does not encourage mixed marriages, because they can be a danger to the faith of the Catholic person and especially of the children. However, the Church allows a mixed marriage for good reasons, but only under certain conditions.

The conditions required before permission is given for a mixed marriage are:

1. The Catholic party has to make a special declaration of his or her fidelity to the Catholic Faith and promise to do everything possible to have the children baptized and brought up in the Catholic Faith.

2. The non-Catholic party is to be fully informed of the obligations of the Catholic partner.

The **bond** of Christian Marriage cannot be broken, except by the death of husband or wife. Our Lord taught: "**So they are no longer two but one flesh. What therefore God has joined together let no man put asunder.**" (Matthew 19:6).

Therefore the Church cannot marry persons divorced from a living lawful husband or wife. If these people marry again outside the Catholic Church, they are not separated from the Church, but they cannot receive the Eucharist until they go to see a priest and fulfil certain conditions.

In the Sacrament of Marriage, husband and wife receive a special Grace:

1. to be "one" together;
2. to remain faithful to one another;
3. to welcome God's gift of children.

The Grace of Marriage helps parents to bring up their children in true reverence and love of God. Each Christian family is a "domestic church", that is, a community of grace and prayer, a school of human virtues and of Christian charity.

Sacramentals

We use sacramentals. These are Catholic signs, symbols and customs which do not confer grace, but help us to receive grace. Some sacramentals are: using holy water, blessed ashes or candles or wearing a crucifix, medal or scapular.

Christian Funerals

When we celebrate Christian funerals, we express our faith in the Resurrection of Christ and our hope of eternal life. We offer the funeral Mass to gain repose for the dead and comfort for the living. We reverence the body of the deceased with a final farewell, in the prayerful hope that we will meet again in heaven.

Part III. WE LIVE IN CHRIST

God calls us to live in his friendship. God has made us in his own image and likeness. God wants us to be happy in this life and the next (see No. 3 and No. 4).

21. CREATED TO BE HAPPY AND FREE

Jesus Christ taught us how to be happy in this life and the next by showing us how happy are those who live according to God's will. We call his teaching the Beatitudes because each sentence begins with the word "blessed" (Latin, beatus). By "blessed" we mean enjoying true and lasting happiness which only comes from God.

The Beatitudes

Jesus Christ taught:

"Blessed are the poor in spirit, for theirs is the kingdom of heaven.
Blessed are those who mourn, for they shall be comforted.
Blessed are the meek, for they shall inherit the earth.
Blessed are those who hunger and thirst for righteousness, for they shall be satisfied.
Blessed are the merciful, for they shall obtain mercy.
Blessed are the pure in heart, for they shall see God.
Blessed are the peacemakers, for they shall be called sons of God.
Blessed are those who are persecuted for righteousness' sake, for theirs is the kingdom of heaven.

Blessed are you when men revile you and persecute you and utter all kinds of evil against you falsely on my account. Rejoice and be glad, for your reward will be great in heaven." (Matthew 5:3-12)

The Beatitudes call us to choose to be good and happy. Because they lived according to the Beatitudes, the saints are already blessed. We want to be blessed like them. We want to enjoy eternal life with them. God has made me to desire his perfect happiness.

God made me to know Him, love Him and serve Him here on earth and to be happy with Him forever in heaven.

Man's Freedom

God created me to seek this happiness with Him freely.

I have **free-will** (see No. 4). In my mind and will I have the power to do something or not to do something. I can choose between good and evil. I can choose what is right or I can choose what is wrong.

God made me to be responsible for what I do. Sometimes I do not act freely, because I am: ignorant, careless, forced along, frightened, weak, foolish or confused. My freedom is limited by sin, and the effects of original sin in me (Romans 7:13-25 and see No. 4).

I have a right to be free to do what is good and to practise my religion. Society should recognize this freedom to practise religion. But I do not have a right to say or do anything I like.

God alone makes me truly free, as his son or daughter through Grace (Romans 8:21; Galatians 5:1; and see No. 27).

22. RIGHT AND WRONG

Because I am a free person, I am responsible for what I do in this world. My actions are either right or wrong, good or bad.

A human act is good or bad depending on:

1. what **I choose** to do, whether it is something good or evil;

2. what **I intend** to do, whether I plan or wish good or evil;

3. The **circumstances**, which may affect how freely I act.

Good intentions or the circumstances cannot make something evil become something good.

Before I act, I must know how to do good and avoid evil. Often I think I know right from wrong through emotions or strong feelings. Emotions are not a sure guide.

Moral Conscience

My sure guide is deep within my heart and mind. I can know right from wrong through using my conscience.

My conscience is my moral judgement, guiding me to choose right from wrong. I must always follow my conscience.

I must first **form** my conscience through faith, prayer and self-examination and through learning the moral teachings of Jesus Christ and his Church. Moral teachings are contained in the Commandments God has revealed to us and in the Commandments of his Church. I also form my conscience by training and practice each day.

My conscience can be guided by some unchanging moral truths:

1. you may never do evil so that good may result from it.

2. the Golden Rule: "**Whatever you wish that others would do to you, do so to them.**" (Matthew 7:12; Luke 6:31).

3. respect and love those around you and never make them do what is wrong.

My conscience can fall into error, if I am ignorant. It can be my fault if I am ignorant, for example, if I do not bother to learn the teaching of Christ and his Church. It would not be my fault if I did not know any better, for example, because no one had ever taught me the truths of our Faith. Day by day, I must form my conscience through faith, prayer and practice (1 Timothy 1:5; 1 Peter 3:21).

23. VIRTUES

The Virtues are good habits which strengthen the conscience and help us to do good and live well. There are two main kinds of Virtues: Human and Theological.

The Human Virtues

The Human Virtues are the good habits that we develop and maintain through our own efforts. We call these Virtues "cardinal" because they are the hinges on which human goodness depends.

The four **Cardinal Virtues** are Prudence, Justice, Fortitude and Temperance (Wisdom 8:7).

1. **Prudence** enables me to judge and choose carefully what is right and good in my life.

2. **Justice** enables me to be fair and honest, treating others as I would want them to treat me.

3. **Fortitude** enables me to overcome temptation, to conquer fear and face suffering bravely.

4. **Temperance** enables me to be balanced and moderate in using created things, such as food and drink.

We maintain and develop these virtues in our lives through effort, education and doing good. But we need the Grace of God through prayer and the Sacraments to follow what is good and avoid evil.

The Theological Virtues

God the Holy Spirit gives us the higher Theological Virtues. We call these Virtues "theological" because they are the direct Gift of God and are not the fruit of our efforts.

The three **Theological Virtues** are Faith, Hope and Charity (1 Corinthians 13).

1. **Faith** enables me to believe in God and all that has been revealed by God. I make an act of Faith to show that I firmly believe in God and all the truths that God has taught.

2. **Hope** enables me to face the future, confidently trusting in God and wanting to be with Him forever. I make an act of Hope to show that I desire eternal life, and the means to obtain eternal life with God.

3. **Charity** (Love) enables me to love God and to love my neighbour as myself. I make an act of Love to show that I love God above all for His own sake, and my neighbour as myself for the love of God (Acts of Faith Hope and Charity, (see **Prayers**, no. 32).

The Gifts and Fruits of the Holy Spirit

God the Holy Spirit gives us his own higher Gifts so that we can live holy and moral lives.

The seven Gifts of the Holy Spirit are:

Wisdom, Understanding, Counsel, Fortitude, Knowledge,

Piety, Fear of the Lord.

We receive these Gifts in the Sacrament of Confirmation (see No. 15).

These Gifts bear beautiful fruits in a happy moral and spiritual life.

The twelve **Fruits of the Holy Spirit** are:

Charity, Joy, Peace, Patience, Kindness, Goodness, Faithfulness, Gentleness, Faith, Modesty, Continence, Chastity (Galatians 5:22).

24. SIN

Members of the Church, like all people, can still do wrong. Sin is any wilful thought, word, deed or failure to do something, which is an offence against the love and law of God. Sin is disobedience, a revolt against God (Genesis 3:5), which harms us and sets us against one another.

In the face of our sins, God is merciful. Jesus Christ came to save us from our sins, to free us from guilt and suffering, and to call us to conversion (Mark 1:14,15).

In our life of conversion from sin, we learn that there are two different levels of sin: **mortal sin** and **venial sin**.

1. Mortal Sin

When we break God's law in a serious way, this is mortal sin (1 John 5:16-17).

I commit a mortal sin when I knowingly and willingly consent to do something which I believe to be a mortal sin.

By mortal sin my soul rebels against God. I lose Sanctifying Grace and all right to heaven. To commit a mortal sin is the greatest of all evils.

If I commit a mortal sin, I should at once make an act of perfect contrition (See **Prayers**, No. 32), and then go to

Confession as soon as I reasonably can.

Perfect Contrition is sorrow for our sins because they offend God who is so good Himself and deserves to be loved so much by us. Perfect Contrition immediately takes away sins by giving Sanctifying Grace (see No. 27), and restores us to God's friendship even before we go to Confession.

But when we go to Confession, we are bound to tell all the mortal sins we can remember which have not been already confessed and forgiven in the Sacrament of Penance (see No. 18 and **Prayers**, No. 34). Then we are sure of God's forgiveness.

Those who die in mortal sin are lost in hell forever.

2. Venial Sin

When we break God's law in a less serious way than mortal sin, this is **venial sin**.

I commit a venial sin when I knowingly and willingly consent to do something which I believe to be a venial sin.

By venial sin my love for God is lessened, and so I am in greater danger of falling into mortal sin. Receiving the Eucharist, acts of charity and prayer take away venial sins.

The Spread of Sin

As people repeatedly commit sins, vice spreads throughout the world. But the spread of sin cannot totally destroy our sense of right and wrong.

Some sins are particularly harmful because they lead to other sins.

The seven **Capital** (or source) Sins are:

Pride, Covetousness, Lust, Anger, Gluttony, Envy and Sloth.

The four sins **crying to heaven for vengeance** are:
Wilful Murder, the Sin of Sodom, Oppression of the Poor, Defrauding labourers of their wages (Genesis 4; Genesis 18; Exodus 2; James 5).

It is a sin to cooperate with others when they commit sins:

1. by sharing in their sins directly and voluntarily;
2. by ordering, advising, praising or approving them;
3. by not disclosing or hindering sinners when we are obliged to do so;
4. by protecting evil-doers.

Through repeated personal sins, human society itself can develop structures of sin which offend the goodness of God by causing great injustice and suffering.

25. THE HUMAN COMMUNITY

We have been created, in the image of God the Holy Trinity, to live together in society. By their Baptism, Christians are called to play an active role in making society better. The family is the natural basic living cell of society. The human person should be at the centre of society and all social organizations.

The authority of the State is to be respected but according to subsidiarity. By "subsidiarity" we mean that the State, or any large body, must not take over projects which smaller groups, such as the family, or individuals carry out well. The State should serve people in society by always promoting truth, morality and freedom.

Seeking the Common Good

Good Authority in society comes from God (Romans 13:1-2;

1 Peter 2:13-17). Society needs some form of authority. We should obey lawful authority, but the leaders of society are first bound to obey God's moral law (see No. 26).

Everyone is called to seek and serve the common good. By the "common good" we mean what best benefits everyone. The common good is based on:

1 respect for every person;

2. social well-being and development;

3. peace and security for all citizens.

We are called to seek the universal common good, working to help all the people in the world to enjoy peace and justice.

Seeking Social Justice

The Gospel of Jesus Christ calls us to promote social justice, especially on behalf of those who are poor and weak (Matthew 25:40). Social justice is based on the common good and the just use of authority. There are three main principles of social justice, which follow from one another.

1. **Every person is conceived and born with human dignity**. Everyone enjoys rights which flow from this innate dignity of being persons. We must respect other people and their rights and dignity, which must never be taken from them.

2. **Created in the image of God, all people are equal in nature, origin and divine destiny**. People are also different from one another. We must never discriminate against others because of sex, race, colour, social conditions, language or religion. Good differences should be respected. But sinful differences, such as a wide inequality between rich and poor, should be eliminated.

3. **We must strive to practice Solidarity**. By "solidarity"

we mean active charity towards others in society, for example, by just distribution of goods, paying a just wage and settling disputes fairly. We should also practice solidarity between nations. Solidarity includes sharing spiritual goods (Matthew 6:33 and see No. 10).

We should learn and follow the social teachings of the Catholic Church.

26. THE MORAL LAW

We need a moral law to teach us what is right and wrong, to form our consciences and guide us in the right path. The moral law has three levels: 1. the **Natural Moral Law**, 2. the **Old Law** and 3. the **New Law** of Jesus Christ.

1. The Natural Moral Law

God has written His moral law in our human nature (Romans 2:14-16), This moral law in human nature is called the **Natural Law**. It tells us that good is to be done and evil avoided. It is found within the reason of all people and it can never change. But we do not always understand its truths because we are fallen and sinful. We need the light of God's revelation to understand the moral law.

2. The Old Law

God revealed his moral law to Moses in the Ten Commandments (see No. 29). The Ten Commandments show us clear truths of the Natural Law. This is the **Old Law**, set out in books of the Old Testament. It was also a solemn agreement, the **Old Covenant**, between God and his People Israel.

The Old Law was not a perfect moral law, but it was a "teacher" preparing the way for the highest moral law, revealed in Jesus Christ.

3. The New Law of Jesus Christ

Jesus Christ reveals the highest moral law, the **New Law** of his Gospel. The New Law is set out in the Gospels and books of the New Testament. It is also the solemn agreement, the **New Covenant**, revealed in Jesus Christ and sealed by his blood, shed for us on the cross and offered in the Eucharist (see No. 16).

The New Law is the gift of the Holy Spirit which perfects the Old Law. It includes the Ten Commandments, but Our Lord goes further. We must love even our enemies: "**Love your enemies, do good to those who hate you, bless those who curse you, pray for those who abuse you.**" (Luke 6:27). Jesus Christ gave his New Law of love, when he said: "**Love one another as I have loved you.**" (John 15:12 and see No. 29).

27. GRACE AND JUSTIFICATION
Grace and Justification

Grace is the supernatural Gift which God gives us to raise us into his Life, to make us holy and to help us to save our souls. The word "grace" means a free gift.

Without Grace we can do nothing to merit heaven. Speaking of our union with him Our Lord said: "**I am the vine, you are the branches. He who abides in me, and I in him, he it is that bears much fruit, for apart from me you can do nothing.**" (John 15:5). We receive the Grace of God in two ways, as **Sanctifying Grace** and as **Actual Grace**.

1. Sanctifying Grace

The Grace of the Holy Spirit is Sanctifying Grace. When we

receive Sanctifying Grace in the Sacrament of Baptism, we are justified. By saying that "we are justified" we mean that:

1. we are converted and cleansed from our sins (Romans 6:19, 22);

2. through faith, we receive the justice (loving righteousness) of God (Romans 3:26);

3. by this inner conversion we are made pleasing to God;

4. we receive the virtues of Faith, Hope and Charity.

Jesus Christ gained justifying Grace for us by dying on the cross (Romans 3:21-25).

Sanctifying Grace makes us share in the divine life of Christ so that we become the temples of the Holy Spirit, the adopted children of God and heirs to his heavenly Kingdom (John 1:12-18, 17:3; Romans 8:14-17; 2 Peter 1:3-4).

Sanctifying Grace is increased by prayer and good deeds, and especially by offering the Holy Mass, and receiving the Sacraments.

By an increase of Sanctifying Grace our souls become more beautiful and pleasing to God, and by it we gain the right to greater happiness in heaven. Sanctifying Grace is lost by mortal sin and restored by repentance.

2. Actual Grace

We are helped to know and do what is right by Actual Grace, especially at a particular time. We may receive the help of Actual Grace when we pray for guidance and strength in a problem.

Other forms of Grace are special **charisms** (supernatural gifts) (Romans 12:6-8) and the **grace of a particular state** of life which God gives to those he has called to a vocation such as priesthood, religious life or marriage.

We can do nothing by ourselves to merit the justifying Grace of conversion. It is always God's free gift. However, when we are moved by the Holy Spirit, we can merit for ourselves and for others all the graces needed for eternal life and life in this world.

Christian Holiness

All Christians are called to be holy, that is, to be more closely united to Jesus Christ, for he teaches us: "**Be perfect as your heavenly Father is perfect.**" (Matthew 5:48). Only through the Grace of God can we grow in holiness (John 4:14,7; 38-39).

Through his Grace we discipline ourselves and make daily sacrifices, taking up Christ's cross and following him to the end (Matthew 16:24).

Through his Grace we can persevere in the Christian life until death, and so finally enter the eternal glory of Christ's Kingdom (Romans 8:28-30).

The Church, Mother and Teacher

In the communion of the Church, by listening to God's word, we learn how to live according to the law of Christ, helped through the Grace of the Sacraments and the example of Our Lady and the saints.

As Mother and Teacher, the Catholic Church is our sure guide in the moral life. From the apostles, she has received the command of Christ to announce the saving truth (1 Tim 3:15).

The Church can infallibly interpret the natural moral law in the authentic teachings of the Pope and the Bishops in union with him.

28. THE PRECEPTS OF THE CHURCH

We are bound to obey all the commandments of our Mother and Teacher, the Church because, she receives her power to make commandments directly from Jesus Christ. He said: **"He who hears you hears me, and he who rejects you rejects me, and he who rejects me rejects him who sent me."** (Luke 10:16).

The principal commandments or **precepts of the Church** are:

* **To worship at Mass on Sundays and Holy Days of Obligation and not engage unnecessarily in bodily work.**
* **To fast and abstain from meat on the days commanded.**
* **To confess our sins at least once a year.**
* **To receive worthily the Blessed Eucharist each year at Easter or within the appointed time.**
* **To contribute to the support of our pastors, and to the upkeep of Catholic schools and charitable institutions.**
* **To see that our children are taught the Catholic Faith and to educate them, if possible, at Catholic schools.**
* **To observe the laws of the Church regarding the celebration of the Sacrament of Marriage.**

In Australia and New Zealand the **Holy Days of Obligation** are: Christmas Day (December 25th) and the Assumption (August 15th). However, the obligation lapses if August 15th falls on a Saturday or a Monday.

Days of Fast and Abstinence are days on which the Church limits the amount of food a person may eat, and forbids the use of meat. There are two such days – Ash Wednesday and Good Friday.

The Church commands us to fast and abstain because

fasting and abstinence help us to practise self-control and so resist temptation. These acts can also be offered to God in reparation for our sins.

By living according to the precepts of holy Church
1. we grow in Grace and holiness;
2. we carry out Christ's mission to the world;
3. we build up his Church;
4. we hasten the coming of his Kingdom of justice, love and peace.

29. THE COMMANDMENTS OF GOD

We are bound not only to believe what God has taught us but to love and serve Him, "... **faith by itself, if it has no works, is dead.**" (James 2:17). We love and serve God by keeping the Commandments of God and the Commandments of His Church.

Jesus Christ taught the Ten Commandments (Matthew 19:6-12, 18-19). The Ten Commandments are the Decalogue ("ten words") which God first revealed through Moses. The Commandments also express specific truths of the Natural Law (see no. 26).

All Ten Commandments are included in these words: "**You shall love the Lord your God with all your heart, and with all your strength, and with all your mind; and your neighbour as yourself.**" (Luke 10:27).

God gives us his own help, Grace, so that we can not only follow the Commandments of God and his Church but enjoy following them. We need Grace to keep God's Commandments and those of his Church.

The Ten Commandments

God revealed the Ten Commandments, saying: "**1 am the Lord your God,**
1. **You shall not have strange gods before me.**
2. **You shall not take the name of the Lord your God in vain.**

3. Remember to keep holy the Lord's Day.

4. Honour your father and your mother.

5. You shall not kill.

6. You shall not commit adultery.

7. You shall not steal.

8. You shall not bear false witness against your neighbour.

9. You shall not covet your neighbour's wife.

10. You shall not covet your neighbour's goods."

(Exodus 20:2-17; Deuteronomy 5:6-21).

"**You shall love the Lord your God with all your heart, and with all your soul and with all your mind.**" (Matthew 22:37; Luke 10:27). With these words, Jesus Christ summed up the first three of the Ten Commandments.

1. "You shall not have strange gods before me".

We are commanded by the first Commandment to give supreme worship and adoration to God and to God alone (Matthew 4:10). We give supreme worship and adoration to God by the offering of Sacrifice, by prayer, and by acts of Faith, Hope and Love (See **Prayers**, No. 32).

We sin against the first Commandment by turning against the virtues of Faith. Hope and Charity:

1. against Faith, by deliberate doubt, unbelief, heresy or abandoning Christian faith (apostasy);

2. against Hope, by despair, or by presuming to save ourselves or presuming God will forgive us when we do not repent:

3. against Charity, by indifference, ingratitude to God, lukewarmness, spiritual laziness, or hatred of God who loves us so much.

We show our holy Faith in our lives:

1. by learning our religion carefully;
2. by practising it faithfully;
3. by teaching it to others.

We have the right to be free to practice and teach religion in every society. The Catholic Church has the right to spread the Gospel freely in society, based on the unique authority entrusted to her by Jesus Christ. Thus the Church shows forth the kingship of Christ over all creation and in particular over human societies.

We also sin against the first Commandment by taking part in any form of false religion or by superstitious practices such as seances, fortune telling and astrology, all forms of magic or sorcery and by using charms.

Since it denies or rejects the existence of God, atheism is a sin against the first Commandment.

This Commandment teaches us never to worship idols. But we should venerate and respect sacred images representing the true God and his saints. It is lawful and good to honour the Blessed Virgin Mary and the saints, but not to give them divine or supreme honour, which is due to God alone.

2. "You shall not take the name of the Lord your God in vain"

We are commanded by the second Commandment to speak with reverence of God, and of holy persons and things.

We sin against the second Commandment by blaspheming or cursing or by taking oaths that are false, unjust or unnecessary.

This Commandment teaches us to respect our Christian name received in Baptism and to begin our prayers in God's Name: "In the Name of the Father, the Son and the Holy

Spirit", as we make the sign of the cross (see **Prayers**, No. 32).

3. "Remember to keep holy the Lord's Day"

We are commanded by the third Commandment to give special worship to God, at appointed times.

We sin against the third Commandment by wilfully failing to keep Sunday and Holy Days as the Church teaches.

The Church commands us to offer Sacrifice to God on Sundays and certain Holy Days by sharing in the celebration of Mass (Acts 2:42-46; 1 Corinthians 11:17). The Church forbids us to engage unnecessarily in bodily work on these days.

This Commandment teaches us the value of keeping Sunday, the day of the Lord's Resurrection, as a time for prayer, rest and recreation.

"**You shall love your neighbour as yourself**" (Matthew 22:39; Luke 10:27). With these words, Jesus Christ summed up the following seven Commandments.

4. "Honour your father and your mother"

We are commanded by the fourth Commandment to love and honour our parents and superiors, and to obey them in all that is not sinful.

We sin against the fourth Commandment by all contempt, ill-will or disobedience towards our parents or to others placed over us to act for our parents.

Under the fourth Commandment, the chief duties of parents are to provide for their children, to instruct them in Christian doctrine, to send them to Catholic schools, if possible, and by love, care and good example and every means in their power, to bring them to God.

This Commandment teaches us to honour the family, the original cell of social life, to protect its rights and to care for all members of the family, especially children and the elderly. This Commandment also teaches us to honour and respect all who lawfully exercise political and legal authority in society.

5. "You shall not kill"

We are commanded by the fifth Commandment to take proper care of our own life and health, and to live in peace and love with our neighbour. Who is my neighbour? Everyone is my neighbour.

We sin against the fifth Commandment by murder, or by drunkenness, drug abuse, suicide, quarrelling, hatred or revenge.

It is murder deliberately to kill innocent human beings: an unborn child (abortion), or any helpless, old or sick person (euthanasia).

This Commandment teaches us respect the life and the bodily health of others, to safeguard and make peace, and to avoid war.

6. "You shall not commit adultery"

We are commanded by the sixth Commandment to be pure in what we think, say and do: **"Blessed are the pure in heart, for they shall see God."** (Matthew 5:8). The virtue of holy purity, self control and self-giving is called chastity. All the baptized are called to live according to the virtue of chastity.

We sin against the sixth Commandment by deliberately agreeing to impure thoughts, words or actions, alone or with others.

This Commandment teaches us to be faithful to our wife or husband, to reject artificial methods of spacing or preventing childbirth, and not to live together or act as husband and wife without first getting married.

7. "You shall not steal"

We are commanded by the seventh Commandment to be just in our dealings with our neighbour, to pay just wages, and to do honest work. I have a right to own private property, always remembering that God has created all things to be used and shared by the human race.

We sin against the seventh Commandment by unjustly taking or keeping what belongs to others, by cheating, by injuring any person's property, by taking away any person's freedom (slavery and trafficking), or by abusing the environment and the animals created by God for our responsible use.

This Commandment teaches us to love and serve Jesus Christ in the poor (Matthew 25:31-36), especially through practising the works of mercy.

The seven **Corporal Works of Mercy** are: I. to feed the hungry; 2. to give drink to the thirsty; 3. to clothe the naked; 4. to shelter the homeless; 5. to visit the sick; 6. to visit the imprisoned; 7. to bury the dead.

The seven **Spiritual Works of Mercy** are: 1. to convert the sinner; 2. to instruct the ignorant; 3. to counsel the doubtful; 4. to comfort the sorrowful; 5. to bear wrongs patiently; 6. to forgive injuries; 7. to pray for the living and the dead.

8. "You shall not bear false witness against your neighbour"

We are commanded by the eighth Commandment to speak

with truth and charity, for Our Lord has said: **"And as you wish that others should do to you, do so to them."** (Luke 6:31).

We sin against the eighth Commandment by giving false information under oath, by lies and unfair judgement, by speaking unkindly or unjustly of our neighbour, by concealing the truth or revealing solemn secrets, or by failing to make up for harm caused by lies.

This Commandment teaches that truth must be respected in the means of communication, such as radio, television, the internet, the world-wide web, social media and the press.

The truth is always beautiful. It leads us to love the beauty of God's creation, and the beauty of human art, especially the sacred art of the Church.

9. "You shall not covet your neighbour's wife"

We are commanded by the ninth Commandment to keep ourselves pure in thought and desire.

We sin against the ninth Commandment by taking wilful pleasure in evil thoughts, desires or feelings. But bad thoughts, desires or feelings are not sins unless we knowingly and willingly consent to them.

This Commandment teaches us to try to live in purity according to the virtue of chastity, by always relying on the Grace of God.

10. "You shall not covet your neighbour's goods"

We are commanded by the tenth Commandment to be grateful for God's good gifts to us, and to rejoice in our neighbour's welfare.

We sin against the tenth Commandment by desiring to

take or keep wrongfully what belongs to another person, by greed or avarice (being tied to wealth and power), or by envy and jealousy of others.

This Commandment teaches us not to become attached to material things, such as money, property and pleasure. We must desire God above all earthly things and long to see God forever in his glory.

Part IV. WE PRAY

God calls each of us to a life of prayer. To all who truly seek Him, God gives the gift of prayer. He gave us this gift in the prayers and psalms of God's People Israel, then in the life and prayer of Jesus Christ and his holy Church.

30. PRAYER

Prayer is thinking about God, speaking to Him, desiring to love Him, and asking God to give us what we need for soul and body.

We should pray because God created us and He is our loving Father. On Him we depend in all things.

We can always pray by offering to God all our thoughts, words and actions, every morning and every night, and frequently during the day (see Prayers, No. 32). Our prayers are pleasing to God when we trust in his goodness, when we are ready to accept his will, and when we humbly pray in the name of Our Lord Jesus Christ. By his own example, Christ our Lord teaches us how to pray and he hears our prayers.

How We Pray

The five main forms of prayer are:

1. **Blessing and Adoration**: We bless God who blesses us; in humility we adore Him.

2. **Petition**: Through Christ, we seek forgiveness and ask God to supply all our needs.

3. **Intercession**: With Christ, we ask for the needs of

others.

4. **Thanksgiving**: In Christ, we thank God for creating and redeeming us.

5. **Praise**: In the Holy Spirit, we give glory to God in prayer and song. When we celebrate the Sacrifice of the Mass we use all these forms of prayer (see No. 16).

We pray to **God our Father**, in the Holy Name of Jesus.

We pray to **Jesus, his Son**. We want to know him as our personal Saviour, calling on his Holy Name and honouring his Sacred Heart.

We pray to the **Holy Spirit**, for the Spirit lives within us and helps us to pray. We ask the Holy Spirit to guide and teach us in prayer: "Come Holy Spirit, fill the hearts of your faithful and enkindle in them the fire of your love!"

We pray in communion with the **holy Mother of God**, whom we greet frequently with the words of the "Hail Mary" (see **Prayers**, No. 32 and No. 33).

We pray with the help of **servants of prayer**: the saints in heaven, holy men and women on earth, our family and friends and prayer groups.

We pray in **sacred places**, especially in the church, before the Blessed Sacrament. But we can pray anywhere at any time, alone or with others, at home, or joining in the prayer of a monastic community or by making a pilgrimage.

The Life of Prayer

The Christian makes prayer a normal part of his or her life. Each moment, day and week and the special times of the Church Year are times for prayer. In a personal rule of prayer, I should find a place for morning and evening prayer and grace before meals (see **Prayers**, No. 32), for meditation, perhaps the Liturgy of the Hours, always for Sunday Mass.

Each of us prays in his or her own way, but the Church recognizes three main expressions of prayer in our daily lives:

1. **Vocal prayer**: praying aloud, alone or in a group.

2. **Meditation**: directing our minds, imagination and will to God, helped by various methods, for example, reflecting on the Scriptures or praying the rosary.

3. **Contemplative Prayer**: seeking the gift of union with God, in silence deep within the human heart. This is the highest form of prayer which God grants to chosen souls.

I should always be humble and trust God in prayer. I should persevere in prayer, even when it seems difficult, because prayer is an essential part of Christian life. Jesus Christ himself says that we "**ought always to pray and not lose heart**" (Luke 18:1).

31. THE LORD'S PRAYER

Jesus Christ taught us his own prayer, the "**Our Father**". This is the prayer of his Church and it sums up the Gospel of Christ.

We dare to say "Our Father" because we are the Father's adopted children, praying as one family, in union with Jesus Christ His Son.

The Words of the Lord's Prayer

Our Father: As sons and daughters of God, we love, adore and glorify the Father together with the Son and the Holy Spirit.

Who art in heaven: The Father dwells in eternity, which

is our homeland; yet He who is above all things is very close to us, for He lives in our hearts.

In the seven petitions of the Lord's Prayer we strengthen our faith and ask God to provide for our daily needs of body and soul.

1. **Hallowed be thy name**: We enter God's plan and ask that we may grow more in the divine holiness we received in Baptism.

2. **Thy Kingdom come**: We look forward in hope, asking that God's reign will triumph not only at the end of time but here and now in the world.

3. **Thy will be done on earth as it is in heaven**: We ask our Father to unite our will to his Son's will, so that God's saving plan may be carried out in the world.

4. **Give us this day our daily bread**: We ask to be nourished not only in our bodies but in body and soul, through God's word and the Blessed Eucharist.

5. **And forgive us our trespasses as we forgive those who trespass against us**: We ask God to be merciful to us poor sinners and to help us to be able to forgive others who sin against us.

6. **And lead us not into temptation**: We ask God not to allow us to take the paths of sin, but to strengthen us to resist temptations in life's daily struggle.

7. **But deliver us from evil**: We claim the victory of Christ, asking our Father to protect us from the devil, a fallen angel who opposes God and his plan (see No. 4).

At Mass, after the Lord's Prayer, we proclaim the "kingdom, the power and the glory" of our loving Father.

We give our assent to everything contained in the Lord's Prayer when we say: "so be it" — Amen.

32. PRAYERS

The Sign of the Cross

✝ In the name of the Father and of the Son and of the Holy Spirit. Amen.

Our Father, who art in heaven; hallowed be thy Name; thy Kingdom come; thy will be done, on earth as it is in heaven. Give us this day our daily bread, and forgive us our trespasses as we forgive those who trespass against us. And lead us not into temptation but deliver us from evil. Amen.

Hail Mary, full of grace, the Lord is with thee. Blessed art thou amongst women and blessed is the fruit of thy womb, Jesus. Holy Mary, Mother of God, pray for us sinners, now and at the hour of our death. Amen.

The Apostles' Creed:

I believe in God the Father Almighty,
Creator of heaven and earth.
I believe in Jesus Christ, his only Son, our Lord.
He was conceived by the power of the Holy Spirit
and born of the Virgin Mary.
He suffered under Pontius Pilate,
was crucified, died and was buried.
He descended to the dead.
On the third day he rose again.
He ascended into heaven,
and is seated at the right hand of the Father.
He will come again to judge the living and the dead.
I believe in the Holy Spirit,
the Holy Catholic Church,
the communion of saints,

the forgiveness of sins,
the resurrection of the body
and life everlasting. Amen.

Glory be to the Father and to the Son and to the Holy Spirit. As it was in the beginning is now and ever shall be, world without end. Amen.

A Short Act of Contrition:
O my God, I am very sorry that I have sinned against you, because you are so good, and with your help, I will not sin again. Amen.

The Morning Offering:
O Jesus, through the most pure heart of Mary, I offer you the prayers, works, joys and sufferings of this day for all the intentions of your Divine Heart.

Confiteor:
I confess to almighty God
that I have greatly sinned,
in my thoughts and in my words,
in what I have done, and in what I have failed to do,
through my fault, through my fault, through my most grievous fault;
(*Here you may call to mind your sins*)
therefore I ask blessed Mary ever-Virgin,
all the Angels and Saints,
to pray for me to the Lord our God.

May almighty God have mercy on us,
forgive us our sins,
and bring us to everlasting life. Amen.

Act of Faith:

My God, I believe in you and all that your Church teaches, because you have said it, and your word is true.

Act of Hope:

My God, I hope in you, for grace and glory, because of your promises, your mercy and your power.

Act of Charity:

My God, because you are so good, I love you with all my heart, and for your sake, I love my neighbour as myself.

Grace Before and After Meals:

✝ Bless us. O Lord, and these your gifts that we have received from your bounty, through Christ our Lord. Amen.

✝ We give you thanks, Almighty God, for these and all your gifts that we have received from your bounty, through Christ our Lord. Amen.

The Divine Praises:

Blessed be God.
Blessed be his holy Name.
Blessed be Jesus Christ, true God and true man.
Blessed be the Name of Jesus.
Blessed be his most Sacred Heart.
Blessed be his most Precious Blood.
Blessed be Jesus in the most holy Sacrament of the altar.
Blessed be the Holy Spirit, the Paraclete.
Blessed be the great Mother of God, Mary most holy.
Blessed be her holy and Immaculate Conception.
Blessed be her glorious Assumption.

Blessed be the name of Mary Virgin and Mother.
Blessed be Saint Joseph, her most chaste spouse.
Blessed be God in his Angels and in his Saints.

Prayers for the Dead:

℣ Eternal rest grant unto them, O Lord.
℟ And let perpetual light shine on them.
May they rest in peace. Amen.

Have mercy, Lord, on the soul of... May he/she rest in peace. Amen.

Arrow Prayers or Aspirations:

At any time we can make these short prayers of faith and love:

Jesus!

Jesus, I trust in you.

My Lord and my God! (*Suitable at the elevation of the Host and Chalice at Mass.*)

Lord Jesus Christ, Son of God, have mercy on me, a sinner. (*The "Jesus Prayer"; repeated again and again by some Eastern Christians, also a good short act of contrition*)

Most Sacred Heart of Jesus, have mercy on us.

My Jesus mercy, Mary help.

My God and my all.

Come, Holy Spirit.

Lord, I believe. Help my unbelief.

Immaculate heart of Mary, pray for us.

All for you, O my Jesus, all for you.

Mother most pure pray for me.

Jesus, Mary and Joseph. I give you my heart and my soul.

Jesus, Mary and Joseph. Help me now and in the hour of my death.

33. PRAYERS TO OUR LADY

The Angelus:

At morning, noon and evening, we recall the Incarnation as we say:

℣ The Angel of the Lord declared unto Mary

℞ And she conceived by the Holy Spirit.

Hail Mary...

℣ Behold the handmaid of the Lord.

℞ Be it done to me according to your word.

Hail Mary...

℣ And the Word was made flesh.

℞ And dwelt among us.

Hail Mary...

℣ Pray for us, O holy Mother of God.

℞ That we may be made worthy of the promises of Christ.

Let us pray.

Pour forth, we beseech you, O Lord, your grace into our hearts, that we, to whom the Incarnation of Christ your Son was made known through the message of an angel, may by his suffering and Cross be brought to the glory of his Resurrection. We ask this through Christ Our Lord. Amen.

In Easter Season, instead of the Angelus, we say or sing:

Joy to you, O Queen of Heaven. Alleluia!

He whom you were meet to bear. Alleluia!

As he promised, has arisen. Alleluia!

Pour for us to him your prayer. Alleluia!

℣ Rejoice and be glad, O Virgin Mary. Alleluia!

℞ For the Lord has risen indeed. Alleluia!

Let us pray.

O God, you gave joy to the world through the Resurrection of your Son, Our Lord Jesus Christ. Grant that through the prayers of his Virgin Mother Mary, we may obtain the joys of eternal life, through Christ our Lord. Amen.

Praying the Rosary:

We meditate on the Mysteries of the Rosary, thinking about each event in the life of Jesus and May, as we say one Our Father on each large (or separate bead) and ten Hail Marys on the beads gathered in tens (decades).

Joyful Mysteries:
1. the Annunciation by the angel to Mary;
2. the Visitation by Mary to her cousin Elizabeth;
3. the Birth of Jesus at Bethlehem;
4. the Presentation of the Baby Jesus in the Temple;
5. the loss and finding of the Boy Jesus in the Temple.

Luminous Mysteries:
1. the Baptism of our Lord in the Jordan;
2. the marriage at Cana;
3. Our Lord proclaims the Kingdom;
4. the Transfiguration of our Lord;
5. Our Lord institutes the Holy Eucharist.

Sorrowful Mysteries:
1. the Agony of Our Lord in the Garden of Gethsemane;
2. Our Lord is scourged;
3. Our Lord is crowned with thorns;
4. Our Lord carries his Cross to Calvary;
5. Our Lord dies for us on the Cross.

Glorious Mysteries:
1. the Resurrection of Our Lord from the dead;
2. His Ascension into heaven;

3. the Holy Spirit comes upon the Apostles to make the Church;

4. Mary is assumed body and soul into heaven;

5. Mary is crowned Queen of Heaven.

At the end of each decade, we say one Glory be, and it is customary to add: "O My Jesus, forgive us our sins, and save us from the fires of hell. Bring all souls to heaven, especially those who most need your mercy." *At the completion of the Rosary the "Salve Regina" is usually said.*

Salve Regina

Hail, Holy Queen, Mother of mercy! Hail, our life, our sweetness and our hope! To you do we cry, poor banished children of Eve; to you do we send up our sighs, mourning and weeping in this valley of tears. Turn then, most gracious advocate, your eyes of mercy towards us; and after this our exile, show unto us the fruit of your womb, Jesus. O clement, O loving, O sweet Virgin Mary.

Prayer after the Rosary

O God, whose only begotten son by his life, death and resurrection has purchased for us the rewards of eternal life, grant, we beseech you, that meditating on the mysteries of the most holy Rosary of the Blessed Mary ever-virgin, we may imitate what they contain and obtain what they promise. Through Christ Our Lord. Amen.

The Memorare

Remember, O most loving Virgin Mary, that never was it known in any age that anyone who fled to your protection, implored your help or sought your intercession, was abandoned. Inspired by this confidence, we fly to your aid, O Virgin of virgins, our Mother. To you we come, before you we stand, sinful and sorrowful. O Mary, Mother of the Word Incarnate, despise not our petitions but in your mercy hear and answer us. Amen.

34. PRAYERS AT RECONCILIATION
Prayers Before Confession:

Come, Holy Spirit, help me to see my sins, to be sorry for them and to confess them well. (**Read through the Commandments, No. 29, and the Precepts of the Church, No. 28, to help you remember how you have failed to love God and other people by breaking the Law of God and his Church**). Most loving Lord Jesus, I come to this sacrament of peace in trust, not in fear. Mary, my Mother, help me to confess well and to know the pardon and peace of this time of healing. (**When you go to the priest for confession, make the sign of the Cross. Listen to the priest as he welcomes you, then tell him when you last went to confession and confess your sins. He may give some words of advice. He will give you a penance to do. Then say an act of contrition**, see No. 32. **He then gives you absolution. After he has dismissed you, thank him.**)

Prayers After Confession:

Loving Father of mercies, I thank you for your gift of forgiveness. You sent Your only Son to die for me on the Cross. With your Son, you send the Holy Spirit to bring me forgiveness, pardon and peace. Father, I offer you my penance. (**If your penance is a prayer, say it now**) Father, I thank you for the priest who reconciled me today, I thank you for the ministry of the Church. Give us more priests.

Mary, my Mother, help me to know happiness and peace, because God has welcomed me and set me free from my sins. Amen.

35. RECEIVING THE HOLY EUCHARIST
Prayers Before Communion:

Lord Jesus Christ, I believe that you are really here in the holy Sacrament. I believe that you are the living Bread from heaven, my Food and my salvation.

Lord, I hope in you. I trust you. Make me strong. Help me to love you more and never to offend you through sin. I am very sorry for all my sins. Help me to love those around me, to be kind and helpful. Lord Jesus, I love and adore you. I want to receive you in the Holy Eucharist. Mary, my Mother, help me to welcome your Son with joy. (**As you come to the altar, think about Our Lord and pray to him in your own words**).

Prayers After Communion:

Lord Jesus Christ, I thank you for coming to me. You have given me yourself. What can I give you in return? Lord, I give you myself. Use my life for your purposes, as a member of your People, the Church. As you come to each of us, help us all to grow in love for one another. Lord, I especially pray for others... Mary, my Mother, pray for me, that I may receive your Son again soon. (**You may use other prayers, see No. 32**).

* * * * *

God, grant me the serenity to accept the things I cannot change, courage to change the things I can, and wisdom to know the difference.

APPENDIX

A KEY TO THE CATECHISM OF THE CATHOLIC CHURCH

This summary statement is not a catechism, but it leads directly to the appropriate paragraphs of the *Catechism of the Catholic Church*, a deeper and more complete presentation of the truths of the Catholic religion. This great Catechism was prepared in consultation with all the Bishops of the Church and authorized for publication by Pope St John Paul II. It is therefore the most authoritative statement of the Catholic Faith. For ready reference, the sections of this summary statement are linked to the numbers of the paragraphs in the *Catechism of the Catholic Church*. Other important themes are added in brackets.

I   **WE BELIEVE** (the profession of faith, the Apostles' Creed, see no. 32)
1. Faith and Revelation 27-43, 144-175
    The Bible and Tradition 50-66, 74-95, 101-133
2. Principal Truths of Christian Revelation
    The Holy Trinity 232-260
3. God the Creator: Man's Destiny 268-274, 279-314, 325-327
4. Man's Origin: the Fall: the Angels 337-339, 356-379
    The Angels 328-336
    After the Fall of Man 385-412 (the immaculate conception of Mary 488-493)
5. Christ and His Work for Us 422-451
    The Incarnation and Its Purpose 456-463

Jesus Christ, God and Man 464-478

The Life of Jesus Christ (his conception and birth 484-507, his ministry 512-559, his passion and death 571-591, 595-618, 624-628, 631-635, his resurrection 638-655, his ascension 659-664, 668-678)

6. The Holy Spirit 683-690 (symbols of the Holy Spirit 694-701, useful for Confirmation)

The Work of the Holy Spirit 702-741

7. Christ's Church 748-752 (symbols of the Church 753-757)

Founded by Christ 758-769

The Unfailing Church 770-776

1. The People of God 781-786

2. The Body of Christ 787-796

3. The Temple of the Holy Spirit 797-799

8. The Marks of the True Church 811- 812

One 813-822, Holy 823-828, Catholic 830-856, Apostolic 857-865)

9. The Members of the Church 836-838

The Pope and Bishops 874-887, 892-896

The Teaching Church (magisterium) 888-892 and 2032-2040

Christ's Faithful 871-873, 897-933 (the consecrated life 914-933)

Other Christians 818, 838, 1271, 1399, 1400-1401

10. The Communion of Saints 946-959

Mary, Mother of Christ,

Mother of the Church 963-972 and 487-507,721 -726, 773, 2030, (prayer to Mary 2673-2679)

(the forgiveness of sins 976-983 but see no. 17 and no. 24)

11. Death, Heaven, Purgatory, Hell, Judgement (the Resurrection of the Body and Life Everlasting 988-1004, 1020)

1. Death 1005-1014, 1021

2. Heaven 1023-1029 Purgatory 1030-1032
3. Hell 1033-1037
4. Judgement 1Q38-1041 and 668-678
The New Heaven and the New Earth 1042-1050

II   **WE WORSHIP AND CELEBRATE** (the sacraments of faith)

12. The Liturgy 1066-1209 (rite of Mass 1345-1355)
13. The Sacraments 1114-1130, 1210-1211
14. Baptism 1212-1284 (how Baptism is celebrated 1229-1245)
15. Confirmation 1285-1321, 1830-1832
16. Blessed Eucharist 1322-1355 (names of this Sacrament 1328-1332)
     The Eucharist, The Sacrifice 1356-1381 and 1104-1107
     The Eucharist, The Sacrament 1382-1405
17 Penance and Reconciliation 1422-1498 and 976-983, 1846-1869
     Indulgences 1471-1479
18. The Anointing of the Sick 1499-1532 (Viaticum 1524-1525)
19. Holy Orders 1536-1600
     (Bishop 1555-1561, 888-896, Priest 1562-1568, Deacon 1569-1571)
20. Marriage 1601-1666 and 2360-2391
     (Mixed marriages 1633-1637, domestic Church 1655-1658)
     Sacramentals 1667-1676
     Christian Funerals 1680-169

III   **WE LIVE IN CHRIST** (the life of faith)

21. Created to be Happy and Free 1700-1709
     The Beatitudes 17 16-1724
     Man's Freedom 1730-1742
22. Right and Wrong 1749-756, 1762-1 770

Moral Conscience 1 J76-1794

23. Virtues 1803

The Human Virtues 1804-1811

The Theological Virtues 1812-1829

The Gifts and Fruits of the Holy Spirit 1830-1832 and see no. 15

24. Sin 1846-1853 and 976-983 and see no. 17

1. Mortal Sin 1854-1861, 1864

2. Venial Sin 1855,1862-1863

The Spread of Sin 1865-1869

25. The Human Community 1877-1904

Seeking the Common Good 1905-1917

Seeking Social Justice 1928-1942 and 2419-2449

26. The Moral Law 1949-1953

1. The Natural Moral Law 1954-1960

2. The Old Law 1961-7 964

3. The New Law of Jesus Christ 1965-1974

27. Grace and Justification

1. Sanctifying Grace (and justification) 1987-2005, 35, 654

2. Actual Grace 2000 (charisms and grace of state 2003-2004, merit 2006-2011)

Christian Holiness 2012-2016

The Church, Mother and Teacher 2030-2040

28. The Precepts of the Church 2041-2046

29. The Commandments of God 2052-2074

The Ten Commandments 2083

1:- 2084-2132 (magic etc. 2115-2117, atheism 2123-2128, idols 2129-2132)

2:- 2142-2159 (blasphemy, 2146-2148, false oaths, 2150-2155)

3:- 2168-2188 (Sunday obligation 2180-2183)

4:- 2196-2246 (the family 2201-2233)

5:- 2258-2317 (abortion 2270-22275, euthanasia 2276-22 peace and war 2302-2317)

6:- 2331-2391 (birth control 2366-2376, living together and trial marriage 2390-2397)

7:- 2401-2449 (the right to property and theft 2402-2414, respect for the environment 2415-2418, love for the poor 2443-2449)

8:- 2464-2502 (truth and the media 2493-2499, truth, beauty and religious art 2500-2502)

9:- 2514-2427 (purity of heart, thought and desire)

10:- 2534-2550 (materialism, envy, greed)

IV　**WE PRAY** (prayer in the life of faith)

30. Prayer 2558-2623

How We Pray 2624-2696 (forms of prayer 2626-2643, in the Name of Jesus 2665-2668, the Sacred Heart 2669 and 1439, the Holy Spirit 2670-2672, Hail Mary 2673-2679)

The Life of Prayer 2697-2758 (expressions of prayer 2700--2719, persevering in the life of prayer 2725-2751)

31 The Lord's Prayer 2759-2776

The Words of the Lord's Prayer 2777-2865